Canada's
LAND & PEOPLE

PRINCE EDWARD ISLAND

Jennifer Nault

Weigl

CALGARY
www.weigl.com

Published by Weigl Educational Publishers Limited
6325 10 Street SE
Calgary, Alberta T2H 2Z9

Website: www.weigl.com
Copyright ©2008 Weigl Educational Publishers Limited

Library and Archives Canada Cataloguing in Publication

Nault, Jennifer
      Prince Edward Island / Jennifer Nault.

(Canada's land and people)
Includes index.
ISBN 978-1-55388-363-0 (bound)
ISBN 978-1-55388-364-7 (pbk.)

      1. Prince Edward Island--Juvenile literature. I. Title. II. Series.
FC2611.2.N385 2007   j971.7   C2007-902205-7

Printed in the United States of America
1 2 3 4 5 6 7 8 9 0 11 10 09 08 07

Every reasonable effort has been made to trace ownership and to obtain permission to reprint copyright material. The publishers would be pleased to have any errors or omissions brought to their attention so that they may be corrected in subsequent printings.

We acknowledge the financial support of the Government of Canada through the Book Publishing Industry Development Program (BPIDP) for our publishing activities.

Photograph credits: Charlottetown Confederation Centre of the Arts: page 14; Government of PEI Executive Council: page 4 bottom; L.M. Montgomery Collection, Archival and Special Collections, University of Guelph: page 15 top left; The Sir Andrew Macphail Homestead: page 15 middle left; University of Prince Edward Island: page 15 bottom.

Project Coordinator
Heather C. Hudak

Design
Terry Paulhus

All of the Internet URLs given in the book were valid at the time of publication. However, due to the dynamic nature of the Internet, some addresses may have changed, or sites may have ceased to exist since publication. While the author and publisher regret any inconvenience this may cause readers, no responsibility for any such changes can be accepted by either the author or the publisher.

Contents

About Prince Edward Island

Prince Edward Island is located in the Gulf of Saint Lawrence. The island covers 5,660 square kilometres of land. It is Canada's smallest province. Prince Edward Island, New Brunswick, and Nova Scotia form Canada's Maritime Provinces. The Maritime Provinces have water on at least three sides.

In 1799, the British named Prince Edward Island in honour of Prince Edward Augustus, Duke of Kent and Strathern. He was Queen Victoria's father.

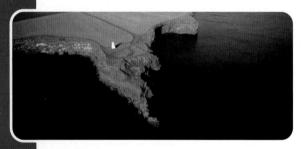

Prince Edward Island's seal was designed in 2002. It shows two foxes to represent natural resources. The blue jay above the shield is the provincial bird. The bird wears a crown to honour the province's ties to Great Britain.

ABOUT THE FLAG

The Prince Edward Island flag became official on March 24, 1964. The flag shows a lion on a red field. The lion stands for British royalty. The large oak tree represents Great Britain. Three small oak trees show Prince Edward Island's three **counties**. The three counties are Kings, Queens, and Prince. The rectangles on the top, bottom, and right sides of the flag are red and white. These are Canada's official colours.

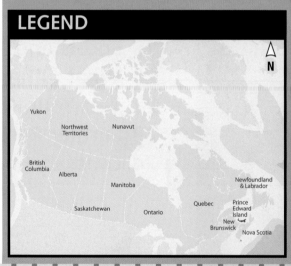

LEGEND

Yukon
Northwest Territories
Nunavut
British Columbia
Alberta
Manitoba
Saskatchewan
Ontario
Quebec
Newfoundland & Labrador
Prince Edward Island
New Brunswick
Nova Scotia

N

ACTION Draw a seal for your family. Include at least three animals, plants, or other items that show what is important to your family. Write a paragraph to explain why you chose those items.

Places to Visit in Prince Edward Island

Prince Edward Island offers many special places to visit and exciting things to do. This map shows just a few. Where would you like to visit in Prince Edward Island? Can you find these places on the map?

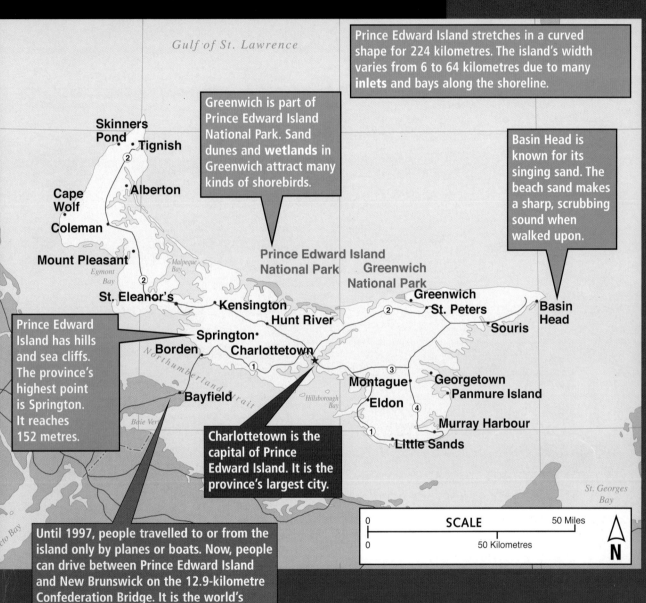

Gulf of St. Lawrence

Prince Edward Island stretches in a curved shape for 224 kilometres. The island's width varies from 6 to 64 kilometres due to many **inlets** and bays along the shoreline.

Greenwich is part of Prince Edward Island National Park. Sand dunes and **wetlands** in Greenwich attract many kinds of shorebirds.

Basin Head is known for its singing sand. The beach sand makes a sharp, scrubbing sound when walked upon.

Skinners Pond
Tignish
Cape Wolf
Alberton
Coleman
Mount Pleasant
Egmont Bay
Malpeque Bay
St. Eleanor's
Kensington
Hunt River
Prince Edward Island National Park
Greenwich National Park
Greenwich
St. Peters
Souris
Basin Head

Prince Edward Island has hills and sea cliffs. The province's highest point is Springton. It reaches 152 metres.

Springton
Borden
Charlottetown
Northumberland Strait
Bayfield
Hillsborough Bay
Baie Ver
Montague
Eldon
Georgetown
Panmure Island
Murray Harbour
Little Sands

Charlottetown is the capital of Prince Edward Island. It is the province's largest city.

cto Bay

Until 1997, people travelled to or from the island only by planes or boats. Now, people can drive between Prince Edward Island and New Brunswick on the 12.9-kilometre Confederation Bridge. It is the world's longest bridge spanning water that freezes in the winter.

St. Georges Bay

0	SCALE	50 Miles
0	50 Kilometres	

N

Beautiful Landscapes

Glaciers covered Prince Edward Island thousands of years ago. They left behind **fertile** soil and red **sandstone** rock. The sandstone's red colour comes from iron oxide, or rust. Tiny bits of sandstone make the soil and some beaches look red or pink. Most of Prince Edward Island's inland area is flat or slightly hilly. The ocean keeps temperatures mild during all four seasons. Average temperatures range from –7° Celsius in January to about 19° C in July. Unlike other Atlantic provinces, Prince Edward Island has very little fog.

Charlottetown soil covers about 190,200 hectares of the island. Its sandy texture is good for growing many crops. The province named Charlottetown soil its official soil in 1997.

Prince Edward Island has many wetlands and small ponds. Laws help protect much of the wetlands from pollution and building that destroys food and homes for wildlife.

In the 1500s, white pine and oak trees covered the island. Settlers cleared much of the forests for farms and shipbuilding. Over time, trees sprouted again. Forests cover about half of the island today.

The northern side of the island has white sandy beaches. Sand dunes and sandbars block many inlets.

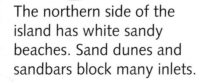

Fur, Feathers, and Flowers

In 1976, Prince Edward Islanders chose the blue jay for the province's bird. This sky-blue bird has black accents on its wings and tail. It lives in Prince Edward Island all year. Geese, duck, partridge, and many other birds live on the island, too. Prince Edward Island has about 333 types of birds. Tourists come to watch many of the birds. Mayflowers, buttercups, and primroses grow in the fields and forests. The wildlife and wildflowers add to the island's natural beauty.

The red oak tree was named the official tree of Prince Edward Island in 1987. The Royalty Oaks Natural Area in Charlottetown preserves these important trees.

Prince Edward Island has many small animals. Mink, foxes, red squirrels, and snowshoe hares live in the forests.

Many creatures, such as seals, fish, and mussels, live in the sea around the island. Sand dollars, sponges, and **moon jellies** also grow near the shores.

The province's official flower is the Lady's Slipper. Its pouch-shaped petals look like slippers. The law does not allow people to pick this type of orchid.

Rich in Resources

Prince Edward Island is called "The Garden Province" and "The Garden of the Gulf" for its rich soil. Soil is the island's main resource. Farmland covers more than half of the island. Today, there are about 1,840 farms in Prince Edward Island. The average farm size is about 142 hectares. Some farms raise cattle, hogs, chicken, and mink. Other farms plant crops, such as potatoes or tobacco. Prince Edward Island's rich red soil and mild weather help the crops to grow well. Tourism and fishing are the province's other main activities.

Potatoes are the island's main crop. Prince Edward Island grows about 1.4 million tonnes of potatoes each year. Farmers sell the potatoes for eating. They also sell **seed potatoes** to more than 20 different countries.

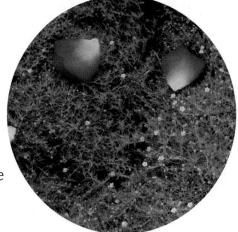

Irish moss grows in the coastal waters around Prince Edward Island. It is a type of seaweed used to thicken products such as ice cream, pie fillings, and toothpaste.

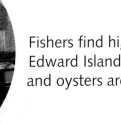

Fishers find high-quality seafood off Prince Edward Island's shores. Lobster, tuna, cod, and oysters are among the valuable catches.

More than 700,000 tourists visit the island each summer. Vacations often include stops at the island's many festivals, historic villages, and sandy beaches. Today, tourism is second only to farming for income.

Shaped by History

Aboriginal Peoples have lived on Prince Edward Island for at least 10,000 years. The Mi'kmaq travelled in birchbark canoes to the island every summer. They lived in **wigwams**. The Mi'kmaq hunted, fished, and gathered food on the island. Then, they moved back to Canada's mainland for the winter. In the 1600s, the Mi'kmaq traded furs for clothing, kettles, and guns from French fur traders. More Europeans came to the area in the 1700s. These settlers brought diseases and changed the Mi'kmaq way of life. Today, about 400 Mi'kmaq live on four **reserves** in Prince Edward Island.

French explorer Jacques Cartier was the first known European on the island. Cartier claimed the island for France in June 1534. Samuel de Champlain claimed the land again for France in 1603.

The French settled the island in the early 1700s. They called the land *Île Saint Jean*, meaning "Island of Saint John." The island was part of an area called **Acadia**, or "land of plenty."

In 1803, Thomas Douglas, Earl of Selkirk, created one of the island's first major Scottish settlements. More people soon followed.

Early settlers were English, Scottish, Irish, and Acadian. Many lived in small log cabins. They farmed, fished, and built ships.

Art and Culture

The Confederation Centre of the Arts in Charlottetown is the largest theatre on Prince Edward Island. The facility has a library and the largest art gallery in the Maritime Provinces. Every summer since 1965, the Confederation Centre of the Arts has presented the musical play *Anne of Green Gables*. It is Canada's longest-running musical. The musical is part of the summer-long Charlottetown Festival. The island hosts about 200 festivals and events each year. Many of them celebrate Prince Edward Island's Scottish, Acadian, Irish, and Aboriginal heritage.

Lucy Maud Montgomery grew up in Prince Edward Island in the late 1800s. She wrote the book *Anne of Green Gables* in 1908. It is a story about a lively orphan girl who moves to a quiet farm in Prince Edward Island. Lucy Maud Montgomery also wrote the patriotic *Island Hymn*, which is the province's official hymn.

The Mi'kmaq hold a powwow at Panmure Island every August. At the powwow they perform drumming and dancing, and eat traditional foods.

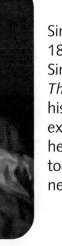

Sir Andrew Macphail was born in Orwell in 1864. He was a doctor, farmer, and author. Sir Macphail was well known for his book *The Master's Wife*. This book was based on his own life in rural Prince Edward Island. His experiments to protect wilderness areas still help scientists study ways to preserve forests today. Visitors can tour Sir Macphail's home near the Orwell Corner Historic Village.

The University of Prince Edward Island is the only university in the province. About 4,100 students attend the university.

Points of Interest

Prince Edward Island treasures its wilderness and scenic beauty. The Prince Edward Island National Park stretches for 40 kilometres from the sea to small inland forests. The park has beaches, cliffs, sand dunes, saltwater marshes, and ponds. Ten provincial wildlife areas in the province protect **habitats** and the creatures that live in them.

Prince Edward Island Park includes the Lucy Maud Montgomery's Cavendish National Historic Site. Visitors can tour the home that inspired *Anne of Green Gables.*

Prince Edward Island set aside about 11,736 hectares of its land for the public to enjoy. Forests cover much of these wilderness areas.

Basin Head Fisheries Museum shows how fishers have made their living from the sea. The province has six other museum and heritage sites across the island. Visitors can learn about shipbuilding, farming, history, and Acadian culture in Prince Edward Island.

In 1864, the "Fathers of Confederation" first met at Province House in Charlottetown. That meeting led to Canada's **Confederation** in 1867. Prince Edward Island became Canada's seventh province on July 1, 1873.

Founders' Hall celebrates the 23 men who met in Charlottetown in 1864. The "Fathers of Confederation" started the nation of Canada.

Sports and Activities

Since 1889, harness racing has thrilled crowds at the Charlottetown Driving Park. Every August, the Gold Cup and Saucer Race attracts some of the best harness racing teams from eastern Canada. Outdoor activities are popular in Prince Edward Island. The province does not have any major-league sports teams. **Amateur** players compete in sports of all types at local schools and recreation centres.

Summer brings deep-sea fishers, sailors, and swimmers to the warm coastal waters off Prince Edward Island. **Kayakers** enjoy exploring the many sandstone inlets.

The Prince Edward Island Rockets play in the Quebec Major Junior Hockey League. Some games are played in Charlottetown.

Golfers can choose from 20 golf courses in Prince Edward Island. The island's courses are well known across North America.

Confederation Trail winds through wetlands, forests, meadows, and small towns. Cyclists, hikers, horseback riders, and joggers can explore 357 kilometres of scenic trails.

What Others Are Saying

Many people have great things to say about Prince Edward Island.

"We were truly amazed at the beauty at every turn of the head. I believe what we saw and experienced was the closest thing to Heaven we have experienced on this planet."

"Rolling farmland contrasts with sand dunes and sandstone cliffs, while sandy beaches compete with evergreen forests and saltwater marshes—there is always something new to explore."

"Prince Edward Island's golf community has a proud history dating back to 1893, when the Charlottetown Golf Club opened its doors. Since then, both the quality and the quantity of golf courses has continued to grow..."

"Over the years, we have learned that to truly appreciate Prince Edward Island, we have to find the roads less travelled, where we slow down and admire the cobalt-blue sky and smell the fresh-mown grass."

ACTION Think about the place where you live. Come up with some words to describe your province, city, or community. Are there rolling hills and deep valleys? Can you see trees or lakes? What are some of the features of the land, people, and buildings that make your home special? Use these words to write a paragraph about the place where you live.

Test Your Knowledge

What have you learned about Prince Edward Island?
Try answering the following questions.

1 What colour is Prince Edward Island's soil? What makes it look that colour?

2 What is the main crop of Prince Edward Island? Why does it grow well there? Visit the library, or surf the Internet to learn more about this crop.

3 Lucy Maud Montgomery is popular for writing which book? Where is the story set? Ask your librarian to help you learn more about Lucy Maud Montgomery and the book.

Try a Potato Stamp

Potatoes are a healthy food grown in Prince Edward Island. Many recipes use potatoes. Ask an adult to help you cut a potato in half. Dip just the white part of the potato into paint. Use the potato to stamp a design on a large piece of paper.

Further Research

Books

To find out more about Prince Edward Island and other Canadian provinces and territories, visit your local library. Most libraries have computers that connect to a database for researching information. If you input a key word, you will be provided with a list of books in the library that contain information on that topic. Non-fiction books are arranged numerically, using their call number. Fiction books are organized alphabetically by the author's last name.

Websites

The World Wide Web is also a good source of information. Reliable websites usually include government sites, educational sites, and online encyclopedias. Visit the following sites to learn more about Prince Edward Island.

Go to the Government of Prince Edward Island's website to learn about the province's government, history, and climate.
www.gov.pe.ca

A Guide to Prince Edward Island is found at
www.peionline.com

For Atlantic Canada Visitor Information, visit
www.atlanticcanada.worldweb.com

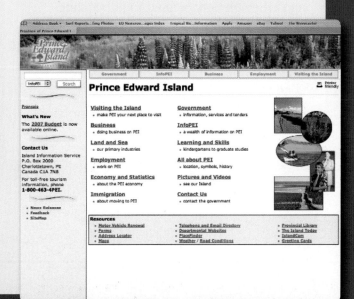

Glossary

Acadia: the name given by the French to their territory in what are now the Maritime Provinces

amateur: a person who plays a game for fun, not for money or a job

Confederation: the coming together of colonies to form the nation of Canada

counties: districts or sections within a province

fertile: good for growing plants

glaciers: large fields of ice that move slowly, often down mountains or along valleys

habitats: places where plants or animals naturally live or grow

inlets: narrow openings of land filled with water

kayakers: people who paddle a type of small, canoe-like boat

moon jellies: common jellyfish that have a clear, round body

reserves: areas of land set apart, usually by treaty, for First Nations peoples

sandstone: a soft rock made millions of years ago when glaciers pressed together sand-sized bits of rock

seed potatoes: potatoes used to plant the next season's crop

wetlands: marshes or swamps

wigwams: tents made of animal skins or bark draped over long poles

Index